Stock Cars

Kate Riggs

seedlings

CREATIVE EDUCATION • CREATIVE PAPERBACKS

Published by Creative Education and Creative Paperbacks
P.O. Box 227, Mankato, Minnesota 56002
Creative Education and Creative Paperbacks are
imprints of The Creative Company
www.thecreativecompany.us

Design by Ellen Huber
Production by Chelsey Luther
Printed in the United States of America

Photographs by Corbis (Chris Crisman), Dreamstime (Walter
Arce, Ashley Dickerson, Ermess, Lawrence Weslowski Jr),
Getty Images (Robert Laberge, Frank Whitney), iStockphoto
(Michael Krinke), Shutterstock (Action Sports Photography,
J5M, Matthew Jacques), SuperStock (Transtock)

Library of Congress Cataloging-in-Publication Data
Riggs, Kate.
Stock cars / Kate Riggs.
p. cm. — (Seedlings)
Summary: A kindergarten-level introduction to stock cars,
covering their speed, drivers, role in racing sports, and such
defining features as their roll cages.
Includes index.
ISBN 978-1-60818-524-5 (hardcover)
ISBN 978-1-62832-124-1 (pbk)
1. Stock cars (Automobiles)—Juvenile literature.
2. Stock car racing—Juvenile literature. I. Title.

TL236.28.R54 2014
629.228—dc23   2014000184

CCSS: RI.K.1, 2, 3, 4, 5, 6, 7;
RI.1.1, 2, 3, 4, 5, 6, 7; RF.K.1, 3; RF.1.1

First Edition
9 8 7 6 5 4 3 2 1

TABLE OF CONTENTS

Time to drive!

Stock cars are
fast race cars.

They go around and
around a track.

The outside of a stock car looks normal. But the inside is not like other cars.

Fast stock cars have powerful engines. They have a roll cage inside the car.

The roll cage keeps the driver safe. Only one person sits in a stock car.

Some stock cars race on superspeedways.

These are

the longest racetracks.

Colorful stock cars drive on a track. They go around a corner.

They head for the finish line!

Go, stock car, go!

Picture a Stock Car

engine

hood

splitter

wheel

steering wheel

roll cage

roof

wing

Office DEPOT

Old Spice

hub

engines: machines inside vehicles that make them move

roll cage: a metal frame to keep a driver safe in case a stock car rolls over

Read More

David, Jack. *Stock Cars*.
Minneapolis: Bellwether Media, 2008.

Mason, Paul. *Stock Cars*.
Mankato, Minn.: Amicus, 2011.

Websites

Bold 'n Bossy Cars Coloring
http://www.yescoloring.com/Cars-Coloring.html
Find pictures of **NASCAR** and other race cars to color.

NASCAR Games
http://www.nascarracinggames.org/
Race cars, put together puzzles, and play other games!

Index